A TRUE BOOK™

My United States

Washington

MELISSA MCDANIEL

Children's Press®
An Imprint of Scholastic Inc.

Content Consultant
James Wolfinger, PhD, Associate Dean and Professor
College of Education, DePaul University, Chicago, Illinois

Library of Congress Cataloging-in-Publication Data
Names: McDaniel, Melissa, 1964– author.
Title: Washington / by Melissa McDaniel.
Description: New York, NY : Children's Press, an imprint of Scholastic Inc., 2018. | Series: A true book | Includes
    bibliographical references and index.
Identifiers: LCCN 2017052797 | ISBN 9780531235843 (library binding) | ISBN 9780531250976 (pbk.)
Subjects: LCSH: Washington (State)—Juvenile literature.
Classification: LCC F891.3 .M37 2018 | DDC 979.7—dc23
LC record available at https://lccn.loc.gov/2017052797

Photographs ©: cover: Edmund Lowe/Alamy Images; back cover ribbon: AliceLiddelle/Getty Images; back cover bottom: Chase
Dekker Wild-Life Images/Getty Images; 3 bottom: BAO imageBROKER/Newscom; 3 map: Jim McMahon/Mapman ®; 4 left:
SteveByland/iStockphoto; 4 right: malerapaso/iStockphoto; 5 top: Derek_Neumann/iStockphoto; 5 bottom: MentalArt/iStock-
photo; 7 top: Derek_Neumann/iStockphoto; 7 center top: JIM BRYANT/UPI/Newscom; 7 center bottom: Jeremy Woodhouse/Getty
Images; 7 bottom: Wolfgang Kaehler/LightRocket/Getty Images; 8-9: dszc/iStockphoto; 11: Gary Braasch/Corbis/Getty Images;
12: zrfphoto/iStockphoto; 13: Chuck Pefley/Alamy Images; 14: Ethan Welty/Aurora Photos; 15: Danita Delimont/Alamy Images;
16-17: fotoguy22/iStockphoto; 19: 400tmax/iStockphoto; 20: Tigatelu/Dreamstime; 22 left: grebeshkovmaxim/Shutterstock; 22
right: railway fx/Shutterstock; 23 top left: SteveByland/iStockphoto; 23 center right: 4x6/iStockphoto; 23 top right: andyKRA-
KOVSKI/iStockphoto; 23 center left: John Glover/Alamy Images; 23 bottom left: malerapaso/iStockphoto; 23 bottom right:
naturediver/iStockphoto; 24-25: Prisma/UIG/Getty Images; 27: Sissie Brimberg/National Geographic/Getty Images; 29: Library of
Congress; 30 bottom right: Art Collection 3/Alamy Images; 30 bottom left: Prisma/UIG/Getty Images; 30 top: Library of Congress;
31 top left: United States. Bureau of Reclamation/Library of Congress; 31 bottom: grebeshkovmaxim/Shutterstock; 31 top right:
Gary Braasch/Corbis/Getty Images; 32: Dan Lamont; 33: Doug Wilson/Corbis/Getty Images; 34-35: David Redfern/Redferns/
Getty Images; 36: Jesse Beals/Icon SMI/Corbis/Getty Images; 37: Bob Pool/Getty Images; 38: Gary Holscher/Getty Images;
39: Stephen Brashear/Getty Images; 40 inset: MentalArt/iStockphoto; 40 background: PepitoPhotos/iStockphoto; 41: Kacey
Klonsky/Getty Images; 42 top left: Paul Fearn/Alamy Images; 42 top right: W.L. Dahl from SPL's Robert T. McDonald Collection/
Seattle Municipal Archive; 42 bottom left: Sergio Gaudenti/Sygma/Getty Images; 42 bottom right: George Rose/Getty Images;
43 top left: Nick Harvey/WireImage/Getty Images; 43 top right: Pictorial Press Ltd/Alamy Images; 43 bottom left: Frank Micelotta
Archive/Getty Images; 43 bottom center: Matt Carr/Getty Images; 43 bottom right: Ron Schwane/AP Images; 44 bottom left:
filonmar/iStockphoto; 44 bottom right: Stephen Brashear/Getty Images; 44 top: ChrisBoswell/Getty Images; 45 center:
sharply_done/iStockphoto; 45 top: Paul Fearn/Alamy Images; 45 bottom: grebeshkovmaxim/Shutterstock.

Maps by Map Hero, Inc.

Scholastic Inc., 557 Broadway, New York, NY 10012

1 2 3 4 5 6 7 8 9 10 R 28 27 26 25 24 23 22 21 20 19

Front cover: Hoh Rain Forest
Back cover: An orca in Puget Sound

Welcome to Washington

Find the Truth!

Everything you are about to read is true **except** for one of the sentences on this page.

Which one is **TRUE**?

T or F Washington is named after a U.S. president.

T or F Washington's state government is divided into two branches.

UNITED STATES

Washington

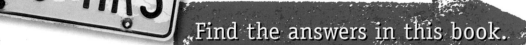

Find the answers in this book.

3

Contents

THE **BIG** TRUTH!

Apple

What Represents Washington?

Willow
goldfinch

4

Seattle skyline

3 History

4 Culture

Cherry pie

This Is Washington!

CANADA

Space Needle

Northwest Museum of Arts & Culture

Strait of Georgia

Strait of Juan de Fuca

BELLINGHAM

Olympic Mountains

Olympic National Park

OLYMPIA

ABERDEEN

Grays Harbor National Wildlife Refuge

SEATTLE

Puget Sound

TACOMA

Washington State Capitol

Mount Rainier National Park

Yakima Electric Railway Museum

YAKIMA

Yakima Valley

Columbia Plateau

Sacajawea State Park

WALLA WALLA

Fort Walla Walla Museum

SPOKANE

WASHINGTON

Cascade Mountains

Okanogan

Columbia

Snake

Snake

PACIFIC OCEAN

Lewis and Clark Interpretive Center

Cowlitz

VANCOUVER

Lewis County Historical Museum

Mount St. Helens Visitor Center

Columbia

Yakima

OREGON

1

2

3

4

N W E S

0   50
Miles

① Space Needle

At 605 feet (184 meters), the Space Needle was the tallest structure in Seattle when it was built for the 1962 World's Fair. Though taller buildings have been built in the city since then, it remains the symbol of Seattle.

② Grays Harbor National Wildlife Refuge

Up to a million plovers, sandpipers, and other birds stop to rest and feed at this spot along the coast. They are taking a break during their long trip from South America to their breeding grounds in the Arctic.

IDAHO

③ Mount Rainier National Park

Ancient forests and high meadows surround Mount Rainier, the tallest peak in Washington. Located in the southwestern part of the state, this mountain was protected as the nation's fifth national park in 1899.

④ Fort Walla Walla Museum

This museum in southeast Washington's Walla Walla shows what life was like in the 1800s for Native Americans, pioneers, and settlers.

Picture Lake in northern Washington got its name from being one of the most photographed areas of the country.

CHAPTER 1

Land and Wildlife

Washington is tucked into the northwestern corner of the **contiguous** United States. It boasts dark, dripping rain forests, cold rushing rivers, and dry, rolling plains. The Cascade Mountains draw a sharp north-south line through the state. Washington's highest peaks are in the Cascade Mountains. These include Mount Rainier, Mount Adams, and Mount St. Helens. Some of these towering, volcanic mountains are covered by snow and ice throughout the year.

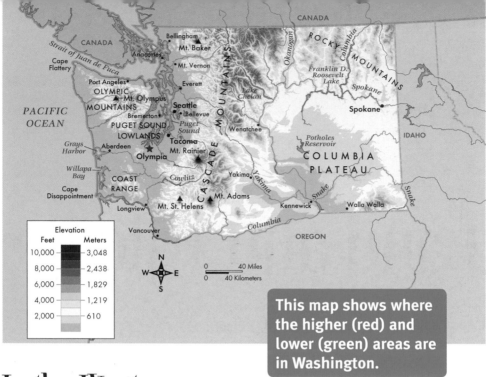

This map shows where the higher (red) and lower (green) areas are in Washington.

In the West

West of the Cascades, the land is lush and green. In the northwest, the jewel-like San Juan Islands dot the bright-blue waters of the **Strait** of Juan de Fuca. This body of water runs between Washington and Canada. To the south, the arms of a body of water called Puget **Sound** reach deep into the state. Ferries ply the sound, connecting Seattle, Edmonds, and other cities to nearby islands. To the west are the dense forests of the Olympic Peninsula.

The Big Boom

On May 18, 1980, Mount St. Helens erupted. The volcanic peak lost about 1,300 feet (396 m) in height as its round top exploded. Ash clogged the air of eastern Washington, turning the bright day dark. It drifted east and fell like snow on cities as far away as Denver, Colorado. Back on the mountain, the blast blew down forests. Mudslides filled rivers. The rich surrounding landscape became a desolate wasteland. Over the years, however, plants and animals have gradually reclaimed the land.

Huge clouds of ash shoot into the sky as Mount St. Helens erupts in 1980.

The narrow, steep canyon walls of Palouse Falls State Park were carved by the Palouse River.

In the East

The Columbia Plateau covers most of southeast Washington. Here, much of the land is dry. The Columbia River, Washington's major river, runs south from Canada through eastern Washington, then turns along the southern border with Oregon. It provides vital water for agriculture. In some parts of the land, rivers have carved out canyons. Near Washington's eastern border with Idaho, the land is mountainous. In the north are the Okanogan Highlands, part of the Rocky Mountains. In the south are the Blue Mountains, which spread into Oregon.

Wet and Dry

When people think of Washington, they often imagine a place where it rains a lot. West of the Cascades, this image is often true. Rain and fog are common. In Seattle, it rains an average of 150 days per year. Eastern Washington is another story. The Cascade Mountains block the clouds coming in off the ocean, so few rain clouds make it to the east. Summer temperatures in the east are hot, frequently topping 100 degrees Fahrenheit (38 degrees Celsius). The weather is usually a bit cooler in the west.

Seattle is a famously rainy city, but its temperatures are usually mild.

MAXIMUM TEMPERATURE 118°F

MINIMUM TEMPERATURE -48°F

Plants

Washington has an amazing array of landscapes that support a wide variety of plants. In the west, Douglas firs and ponderosa pines tower above forests filled with ferns, mushrooms, and delicate flowers. Thick moss carpets the ground and the fallen logs in the wet forests of Olympic National Park. In the east, hardy shrubs such as sagebrush survive in the dry soil.

Rock formations called sea stacks are a common site along the coast of Olympic National Park.

Because they are used to being around boats and people, seals along Washington's coast are not afraid to rest on docks.

Animals

Washington's forests are alive with animals. Deer and elk munch on soft leaves, and black bears hunt for berries. High in the mountains, goats scramble up rocky slopes. Along the coast, eagles soar high overhead, scouring the water for salmon, trout, and other fish. Herons, meanwhile, wade slowly through the shallow water in search of prey. Seals lounge along the rocky shore, while orcas and other whales swim offshore.

Washington's capitol dome is 287 feet (87 m) tall.

LEGISLATIVE

CHAPTER 2

Government

When Washington **Territory** was created in 1853, Olympia was named its capital. At the time, Olympia was home to only about 150 people, yet it was the largest settlement in the territory. It was also centrally located. By the time Washington became a state in 1889, other cities had grown larger than Olympia, but the capital remained in place. Today, the state government is the city's largest employer.

State Government Basics

Like the governments of other states, Washington's government has three branches. The executive branch is responsible for carrying out the state's laws and the day-to-day matters of governing. It is headed by the governor. The legislative branch makes the state laws. It is made up of the Senate and the House of Representatives. The judicial branch consists of the state courts. It holds trials and settles legal disputes.

WASHINGTON'S STATE GOVERNMENT

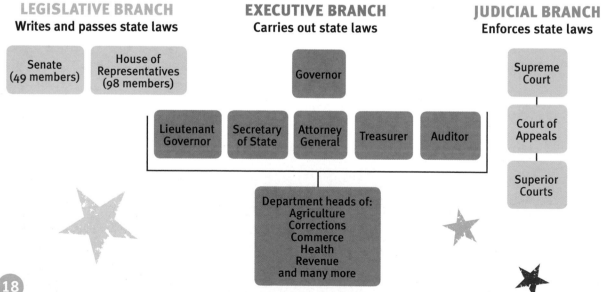

LEGISLATIVE BRANCH
Writes and passes state laws

- Senate (49 members)
- House of Representatives (98 members)

EXECUTIVE BRANCH
Carries out state laws

- Governor
- Lieutenant Governor
- Secretary of State
- Attorney General
- Treasurer
- Auditor

Department heads of:
Agriculture
Corrections
Commerce
Health
Revenue
and many more

JUDICIAL BRANCH
Enforces state laws

- Supreme Court
- Court of Appeals
- Superior Courts

State Politics

In Washington, the Cascade Mountains are both a geographic and a political dividing line. People who live west of the Cascades are more likely to vote for members of the Democratic Party. People in eastern Washington tend to vote for candidates from the Republican Party. Far more people live in western Washington than in eastern Washington. As a result, the state's leaders are usually Democratic.

Washington's National Role

Each state elects officials to represent it in the U.S. Congress. Like every state, Washington has two senators. The U.S. House of Representatives relies on a state's population to determine its numbers. Washington has 10 representatives in the House.

Every four years, states vote on the next U.S. president. Each state is granted a number of electoral votes based on its number of members in Congress. With two senators and 10 representatives, Washington has 12 electoral votes.

2 senators and 10 representatives

12 electoral votes

With 12 electoral votes, Washington's voice in presidential elections is above average compared to other states.

The People of Washington

Elected officials in Washington represent a population with a range of interests, lifestyles, and backgrounds.

Ethnicity (2016 estimates)

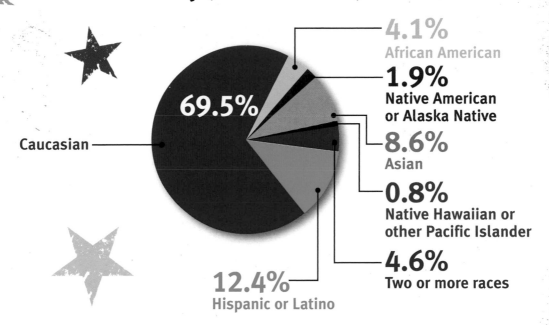

69.5%
Caucasian

4.1%
African American

1.9%
Native American or Alaska Native

8.6%
Asian

0.8%
Native Hawaiian or other Pacific Islander

4.6%
Two or more races

12.4%
Hispanic or Latino

34% have a bachelor's degree or higher.

8% are veterans.

62% own their own homes.

19% speak a language other than English at home.

91% graduated from high school.

14% were born in another country.

THE **BIG** TRUTH!

What Represents Washington?

States choose specific animals, plants, and objects to represent the values and characteristics of the land and its people. Find out why these symbols were chosen to represent Washington or discover surprising curiosities about them.

Seal

Washington's state seal shows a portrait of George Washington encircled by a ring containing the words "The seal of the state of Washington 1889." Washington is the only state named for a U.S. president.

Flag

Washington's state flag displays the state seal against a green background. It was adopted in 1923.

Willow Goldfinch

STATE BIRD

The bright-yellow willow goldfinch was chosen to be Washington's state bird in 1951.

Steelhead Trout

STATE FISH

Steelhead are born in fresh water and move to the ocean as adults. They later return to fresh water to reproduce.

Western Hemlock

STATE TREE

The towering western hemlock is an evergreen tree native to the Northwest coast.

Square Dance

STATE DANCE

Washington's pioneers brought with them a simple folk dance called a square dance. It was named the state dance in 1979.

Apple

STATE FRUIT

Washington produces more apples than any other state.

Pacific Chorus Frog

STATE AMPHIBIAN

Pacific chorus frogs are found in every county in Washington.

The climate was much colder when people first arrived in North America.

CHAPTER 3

History

The first people arrived in what is now Washington long before it became part of the United States. At least 20,000 years ago, people traveled across the Bering Strait between Asia and what is now Alaska. Gradually, they spread out across North America, reaching Washington about 12,000 years ago. Over time, they became experts at hunting, fishing, and growing crops. They settled in different environments and developed many different Native American cultures.

On the Coast

The forests and waters of western Washington provided Native Americans with plenty of food. They hunted whales, collected shellfish, and caught fish. They gathered berries from the forests and built homes using wood from the trees. Because of these rich resources, the people could settle down and develop complex cultures. Generosity was highly valued. People of the Northwest coast held feasts called potlatches. During potlatches, they showered their guests with gifts such as blankets and dried foods.

This map shows some of the major tribes that lived in what is now Washington before Europeans came.

Yakama men dip nets into the Yakima River to catch salmon.

In the East

Native Americans on the eastern side of the Cascades often moved frequently, following herds of bison and other animals. They used every part of the animals they hunted. They turned bison into food, clothing, tools, fuel, tents, and artwork. For many people of eastern Washington, the richest time of the year was when the salmon returned to the rivers to reproduce. So many fish swam upstream that they could easily be scooped up in nets.

European Exploration

In the late 1700s, newcomers began exploring what is now Washington. Russians, Spaniards, British, and others competed in the region's sea otter fur trade. In 1775, Spaniard Bruno de Heceta led a crew ashore. These were the first Europeans to land in Washington. In 1792, a British explorer named George Vancouver mapped the coast. That same year American Robert Gray sailed up the coast and into the mouth of a great river, naming it the Columbia.

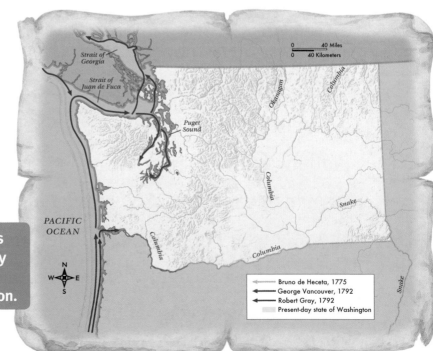

This map shows routes Europeans took as they explored and settled what is now Washington.

Becoming a State

In the 1830s, American traders and **missionaries** began traveling to the Pacific Northwest. By the 1850s, thousands of people were making the long journey each year. One group reached Puget Sound and in 1852 founded a village they named Seattle. Cities in western Washington grew alongside the fishing and logging industries. In eastern Washington, the city of Spokane blossomed as a center for mining, logging, and agriculture. With its economy booming, Washington became a state in 1889.

Hard Times

In 1929, the **stock market** crashed and the **Great Depression** began. All around the country, businesses closed and people lost their jobs. During the 1930s, government programs put some people back to work. In Washington, thousands of workers headed to the Columbia River to build the Grand Coulee Dam and other dams. These dams produced electricity and provided water for **irrigation**.

Timeline of Washington Events

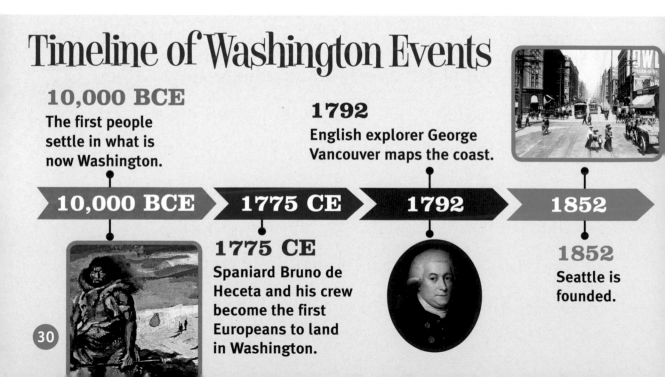

10,000 BCE
The first people settle in what is now Washington.

1792
English explorer George Vancouver maps the coast.

| 10,000 BCE | 1775 CE | 1792 | 1852 |

1775 CE
Spaniard Bruno de Heceta and his crew become the first Europeans to land in Washington.

1852
Seattle is founded.

The Depression didn't end until World War II (1939–1945), when factories began producing military supplies. The United States' enemies in the war included Germany and Japan. Some Americans believed that Japanese Americans would be disloyal. As a result, 13,000 Washingtonians of Japanese descent were forced into **internment** camps. They were imprisoned until the war ended in 1945.

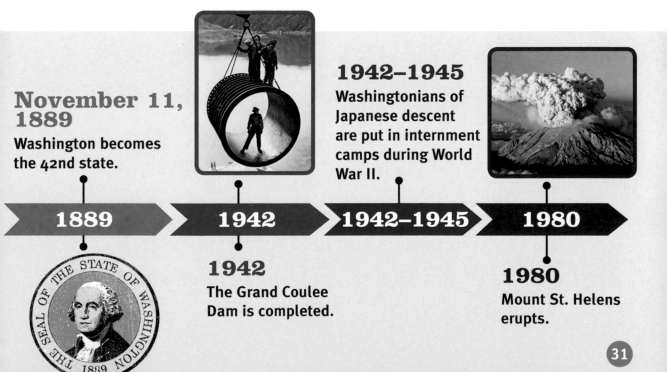

November 11, 1889
Washington becomes the 42nd state.

1942–1945
Washingtonians of Japanese descent are put in internment camps during World War II.

| 1889 | 1942 | 1942–1945 | 1980 |

1942
The Grand Coulee Dam is completed.

1980
Mount St. Helens erupts.

The Port of Tacoma is one of the country's largest shipping ports.

Modern Times

After World War II, Washington's economy grew. Ships carried goods from ports in Puget Sound across the ocean to Asia. As air travel became common, jets built by Seattle-based Boeing winged passengers around the world. In the 1960s, Boeing also built rockets that brought astronauts into space. The excitement for the future was celebrated at a world's fair in Seattle in 1962. Later in the 20th century, Washington continued to lead the way as the home of groundbreaking technology companies such as Microsoft.

Changing Computers— and the World

Bill Gates cofounded the Microsoft Corporation in 1975, and it quickly became a major company. Most computers in the world today use a Microsoft **operating system**. Microsoft, based in Redmond, made the Puget Sound region a technology center. It also made Gates rich. In 2017, he was the richest man in the world. He and his wife have used some of their fortune to help others. The Bill & Melinda Gates Foundation has spent billions of dollars improving health care around the world.

Bill Gates was just 20 years old when he helped found Microsoft.

Jimi Hendrix was inducted into the Rock and Roll Hall of Fame in 1992.

CHAPTER 4

Culture

Washingtonians are big readers. Seattle ranks number one among large American cities in the number of books bought per person. Washington has also had a big influence on rock music. In the 1960s, Seattle-born Jimi Hendrix exploded the idea of what an electric guitar could do. In the 1990s, Washington bands such as Nirvana and Pearl Jam were at the center of the grunge scene. Washington has also been at the center of the art-glass movement. Some of these delicate sculptures can be seen at Tacoma's Museum of Glass.

Jeremy Lane of the Seattle Seahawks shows off the Vince Lombardi Trophy at a parade celebrating the team's 2014 Super Bowl victory.

Play Ball!

Seattle has the only Major League Baseball and pro football teams in the Pacific Northwest. This means fans from all over the region cheer them on. People flock to Safeco Field to watch the Seattle Mariners play baseball. Football fans were thrilled when the Seattle Seahawks won their first Super Bowl in 2014. The Seattle Storm is one of the top teams in the Women's National Basketball Association. Seattle also hosts two pro soccer teams: the Sounders and the Reign.

Celebrations

From east to west, people in Washington love to get together to celebrate. In the east, the city of Wenatchee holds the Washington State Apple Blossom Festival in the spring to honor the state's apple industry. On the coast, people head to Long Beach for the International Kite Festival. But the biggest event of them all is the Washington State Fair in Puyallup. Each year, more than a million people show up to enjoy rides, concerts, contests, and a rodeo.

The International Kite Festival is a week-long celebration held each August.

A Yakima Valley pear farmer inspects his recently harvested crops.

At Work

Washington's earliest industries included logging and fishing, and both remain vital to the state. Farmers grow wheat, barley, and other grains in eastern Washington. Orchards overflow with apples, pears, and cherries. Workers in Washington also build gigantic airplanes and ships, as well as tiny computer parts. Computer software development is a huge industry in western Washington.

High-Tech Jobs

The Puget Sound region in northwestern Washington has become a technology center in recent decades. It is the site of huge companies such as Microsoft and Amazon, as well as many small video game developers and online companies. Thousands of people have moved to Washington to work in these new industries. The state's largest company, however, is still Boeing. About 80,000 people work at the company's facilities in the Seattle area designing and building aircraft.

Workers assemble a massive 787 jet at the Boeing factory in the city of Everett.

Let's Eat

Washington has many rivers and lakes and a long coastline, so salmon, trout, and shellfish are frequently on the menu. Fruits such as apples, cherries, and blackberries are used in many dishes. Washingtonians also love coffee. Starbucks got its start in Seattle.

Cherry Pie

Ask an adult to help you!

Enjoy a tasty pie made from Washington-grown cherries!

Ingredients

¹/₄ cup sugar
¹/₄ cup cornstarch
1 teaspoon vanilla extract
1 tablespoon lemon juice
¹/₈ teaspoon salt

4 cups frozen sweet cherries
2 9-inch pie crusts
1 tablespoon butter, cut into small squares

Directions

Mix the sugar, cornstarch, vanilla, lemon juice, and salt in a large bowl. Add the cherries. Put a pie crust into a pie pan. Pour in the cherry mixture. Sprinkle the bits of butter on top. Then put the second crust on top and trim the sides. Squeeze the edges of the two crusts together. Cut four slits in the top crust to let steam escape. Bake for 20 minutes at 425°F, then reduce the heat to 350°F and bake for another 30 minutes. Let the pie cool for at least 3 hours, then enjoy!

Camping is a great way to get an up-close view of Washington's breathtaking wilderness.

Out and About

Many people move to Washington because they love the great outdoors. Washingtonians take every chance they can to get on the water. They go kayaking, canoeing, sailing, waterskiing, and fishing. They ride their bikes to work and head to the countryside on weekends. Washingtonians also head for the mountains to go hiking, snowboarding, and rock climbing. Whatever type of exploring you prefer, Washington has a lot to offer! ★

Famous People

Seattle (also known as Sealth)

(ca. 1790–1866), was a leader of the Suquamish and Duwamish people. He encouraged peaceful relations between Native Americans and white settlers.

Bertha Knight Landes

(1868–1943) became the mayor of Seattle in 1926. She was the first woman elected mayor of a major U.S. city.

Jacob Lawrence

(1917–2000) was an artist whose paintings often depicted African American life. He lived in Seattle, where he was a professor at the University of Washington.

Chuck Jones

(1912–2002) was an innovative animator known for his Warner Bros. cartoons. He invented such characters as Wile E. Coyote and Pepé Le Pew. He was born in Spokane.

Dale Chihuly

(1941–) is an artist who designs large glass sculptures. He was born in Tacoma.

Jimi Hendrix

(1942–1970) was a legendary rock musician famous for his thrilling guitar solos. He was born in Seattle.

Kurt Cobain

(1967–1994) was a singer and guitarist in the rock band Nirvana, the leading band of the grunge movement of the 1990s. He was born in Aberdeen.

Hilary Swank

(1974–) is an actress who grew up in Bellingham. She has won the Academy Award for Best Actress twice, for *Boys Don't Cry* and *Million Dollar Baby.*

Isaiah Thomas

(1989–) is an All-Star basketball player. At 5 feet 9 inches (1.75 m), he is one of the shortest players ever to play in the NBA. He is from Tacoma.

Did You Know That...

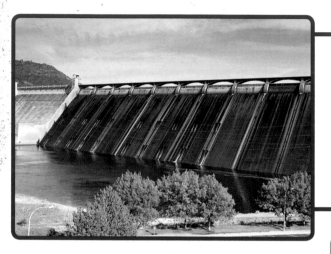

The Grand Coulee Dam is the largest concrete structure in the United States. It contains enough concrete to build a road from Seattle to Miami, Florida.

The Boeing factory in Everett, Washington, is the world's largest building by usable **volume**. In this factory, huge aircraft such as the Boeing 777 airplane are built.

Washington produces about two-thirds of all the sweet cherries grown in the United States.

In 1836, missionaries Narcissa Whitman (pictured) and Eliza Spalding accompanied their husbands on the long, hard trip across the Great Plains and Rocky Mountains to what is now Washington. They were the first white women to complete the overland trip to the Pacific Northwest.

Calculating the length of a coastline is tricky. The answer can vary greatly depending on how carefully every inlet is measured. By one measure, the Washington coastline is 157 miles (253 kilometers) long. By another, it stretches 3,026 miles (4,870 km).

Did you find the truth?

T Washington is named after a U.S. president.

F Washington's state government is divided into two branches.

Resources

Books

Cohen, Fiona. *Curious Kids Nature Guide: Explore the Amazing Outdoors of the Pacific Northwest.* Seattle: Little Bigfoot, 2017.

Demuth, Patricia Brennan. *Who Is Bill Gates?* New York: Penguin, 2014.

Meinking, Mary. *What's Great About Washington?* Minneapolis: Lerner Publications, 2015.

Rozett, Louise (ed.). *Fast Facts About the 50 States: Plus Puerto Rico and Washington, D.C.* New York: Children's Press, 2010.

Tarshis, Lauren. *I Survived the Eruption of Mount St. Helens, 1980.* New York: Scholastic, 2016.

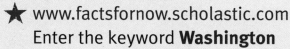

Visit this Scholastic website for more information on Washington:

★ www.factsfornow.scholastic.com
Enter the keyword **Washington**

Important Words

contiguous (kun-TIG-yuh-wus) touching in an unbroken series

Great Depression (GRAYT dih-PRESH-uhn) a worldwide economic crisis that took place mostly during the 1930s

internment (in-TURN-muhnt) confinement during a war

irrigation (ir-uh-GAY-shuhn) the process of supplying water to crops by artificial means, such as channels and pipes

missionaries (MISH-uh-ner-eez) people who are sent to a foreign country to teach about religion and do good works

operating system (AH-puh-ray-ting SIS-tuhm) the software in a computer that supports all the programs that run on it

sound (SOUND) a long, narrow arm of water connecting two bodies of water or separating the mainland from an island

stock market (STAHK MAHR-kit) the system for buying and selling shares of companies

strait (STRAYT) a narrow strip of water that connects two larger bodies of water

territory (TER-ih-tor-ee) an area connected with or owned by a country that is outside the country's main borders

volume (VAHL-yoom) the amount of space taken up by a three-dimensional object

Index

Page numbers in **bold** indicate illustrations.

About the Author

Melissa McDaniel is a writer and editor who was born in Portland, Oregon, just across the Columbia River from Vancouver, Washington. A graduate of both Portland State University and the University of Washington, she now lives in New York City.